M. B Aylsworth

Illustrating Buildings and Faculties of the University of Toronto and Affiliated Colleges

M. B Aylsworth

Illustrating Buildings and Faculties of the University of Toronto and Affiliated Colleges

ISBN/EAN: 9783741124273

Manufactured in Europe, USA, Canada, Australia, Japa

Cover: Foto ©Suzi / pixelio.de

Manufactured and distributed by brebook publishing software
(www.brebook.com)

M. B Aylsworth

Illustrating Buildings and Faculties of the University of Toronto and Affiliated Colleges

ALUMNI SOUVENIR

ILLUSTRATING

BUILDINGS AND FACULTIES

OF THE

University of Toronto

AND

AFFILIATED COLLEGES

ARTS AND DIVINITY EDITION.

COMPILED AND PUBLISHED BY

M. B. AYLSWORTH, ARCHITECT,

CANADA LIFE BUILDING TORONTO

THE SCOPE OF THIS COLLECTION IS LIMITED TO THE CONFEDERATION OF COLLEGES ACKNOWLEDGING FOR THEIR HEAD THE UNIVERSITY OF TORONTO, RESERVING FOR LATER TREATMENT THOSE EXCELLENT INSTITUTIONS REMAINING INDEPENDENT.

THIS EDITION IS FURTHER LIMITED, GIVING THE FULL FACULTY ONLY IN ARTS AND DIVINITY, A SIMILAR EDITION BEING PROPOSED FOR THOSE INTERESTED IN MEDICINE, PHARMACY, DENTISTRY, MUSIC AND AGRICULTURE.

STILL ANOTHER EDITION IS CONTEMPLATED, TO EMBRACE ONLY THE BUILDINGS OF THE MORE IMPORTANT EDUCATIONAL INSTITUTIONS OF TORONTO.

IT HAS BEEN THE AIM OF THE COMPILER TO EXHIBIT HEREIN THE HIGHEST GRADE OF TORONTO WORKMANSHIP, AND HE IS PLEASED TO NAME THOSE WHOSE EFFORTS HAVE BEEN SO CREDITABLE:

THE ENGRAVING, KNOWN AS THE HALF-TONE PROCESS OF PHOTO-ETCHING ON COPPER, IS BY THE GRIP CO.

THE PRINTING ON COATED PAPER BY MR. R. G. McLEAN.

THE BINDING BY BROWN BROS.

THE PHOTOS ARE MOSTLY BY MR. J. BRUCE, THOUGH WARMEST THANKS ARE EXTENDED TO THOSE FEW PROFESSORS, WHO IN EACH CASE REQUIRED, SO READILY LOANED THEIR PHOTOS ON REQUEST.

M. B. A.

NORMAN ENTRANCE.
UNIVERSITY COLLEGE.

Beadle "McKIM."
(Died Aug. 6th, 1892.)

UNIVERSITY COLLEGE.
Built, 1859. Burned, 1890. Restored, 1892.

JAMES BREBNER, B.A.,   J. E. BERKELEY SMITH, Esq.,
Registrar of the University   Bursar of the University.

UNIVERSITY LIBRARY BUILDING   HUGH H. LANGTON, B.A.,
Erected 1892.   Librarian of the University.

JAMES LOUDON, M.A.,
President of the University and of University College,
Professor of Physics.

HON. EDWARD BLAKE, M.A., Q.C., LL.D., M.P.,
Chancellor of the University.

WM. MULOCK, M.A., Q.C., M.P.
Vice-Chancellor of the University.

HON. G. W. ROSS, LL.D., M.P.P.
Minister of Education.

REV. JOHN McCAUL, LL.D.,
Ex-President, 1849-1881.
(Died 1881.)

SIR DANIEL WILSON, LL.D., F.R.S.E.,
Ex-President, 1881-1892.
(Died 1892.)

REV. N. S. BURWASH, S.T.D., LL.D.
President of Victoria College,
Professor of Civil Polity.

R. RAMSAY WRIGHT, M.A., B. Sc.
Professor of Biology.

EDWARD J. CHAPMAN, Ph.D., LL.D.,
Professor of Geology.

ALFRED BAKER, M.A.,
Professor of Mathematics.

JAMES GIBSON HUME, M.A., Ph.D.,
Professor of Ethics and of the
History of Philosophy.

W. H. PIKE, M.A., Ph.D.,
Professor of Chemistry.

JAMES M. BALDWIN, M.A., Ph.D.,
Professor of Philosophy.

W. H. FRASER, B.A.,
Asst. Prof. of Italian and Spanish.

A. B. McCALLUM, B.A., M.B., Ph.D.,
Asst. Prof. of Physiology.

T. R. ROSEBRUGH, B.A., Grad. S.P.S.,
Lecturer in Electrical Engineering.

L. B. STEWART, P.L.S , D.T.S.,
Lecturer in Surveying.

J. GALBRAITH, M.A., Assoc. M. Inst. C.E.,
Principal of the School of Practical Science,
Professor of Engineering.

SCHOOL OF PRACTICAL SCIENCE,
Queen's Park, Toronto.

WYCLIFFE COLLEGE,
Queen's Park, Toronto,

JANITOR "BOB."

VICTORIA COLLEGE,
Queen's Park, Toronto.

FACULTY OF VICTORIA COLLEGE.

REV. ALFRED H. REYNAR, M.A., LL.D.,
Professor of English Literature.

A. R. BAIN, M.A., LL.D.,
Professor of Ancient History.

A. J. BELL, Ph.D.,
Professor of Latin.

JOHN PETCH, M.A.,
Professor of French.

REV. E. J. BADGELY, M.A., LL.D.,
Professor of Mental and Moral Philosophy.

REV. F. H. WALLACE, M.A., B.D.,
Professor of New Testament Exegesis.

REV. J. McLAUGHLIN, M.A., B.D.,
Professor of Oriental Languages.

L. E. HORNING, M.A., Ph.D.,
Professor of German and Old English.

REV. JOHN BURWASH, M.A., D.Sc.,
Professor of Practical Theology.

WYCLIFFE COLLEGE FACULTY.

REV. GUS. ADOLF KUHRING,
Dean in Residence,

REV. F. H. DuVERNET,
Professor of Homiletics.

REV. JAMES PATERSON SHERATON, D.D.,
Principal Wycliffe College,
Professor of Systematic Theology.

REV. GEORGE M. WRONG, B.A.,
Professor of Apologetics and Liturgics,

KNOX COLLEGE FACULTY.

REV. WM. McLAREN, D.D.,
Professor of Systematic Theology.

REV. WM CAVEN, D.D.,
Principal of Knox College. Professor of Exegetics

REV. WILLIAM GREGG, D.D.,
Professor of Church History.

REV. R. Y. THOMSON, M.A., B.D.,
Professor of Apologetics and
Old Testament Literature

REV. J. J. A. PROUDFOOT, D.D.,
Lecturer in Homiletics and
Pastoral Theology.

KNOX COLLEGE.

ONTARIO COLLEGE OF PHARMACY,
Gerrard St. East, Toronto.

MEDICAL ASSOCIATION BUILDING,
Cor. Bay and Richmond Sts.,
Toronto.

A. Y. SCOTT, B.A., M.D.,
Principal of the Ontario College
of Pharmacy.

REV. FATHER JOHN R. TEEFY, B.A.,
Superior of St. Michael's College.

ST. BASIL'S CHURCH AND ST. MICHAEL'S COLLEGE,
St. Joseph Street, Toronto.

W. T. AIKINS, M.D., LL.D.,
Dean of the Medical Faculty of the University of Toronto,
Professor of Surgery.

WALTER B. GEIKIE, M.D., C.M., D.C.L., F.R.C.S., Ed., L.R.C.P., London, Eng.,
Dean of Trinity Medical College,
Professor of Medicine and Clinical Medicine.

VICTORIA HOSPITAL FOR SICK CHILDREN,
College Street, Toronto.

TORONTO SCHOOL OF MEDICINE,   TRINITY MEDICAL COLLEGE,
Gerrard Street East, Toronto.   Spruce Street, Toronto.

TORONTO GENERAL HOSPITAL,
Gerrard Street East, Toronto.

BIOLOGICAL DEPARTMENT,
University of Toronto,
Queen's Park.

F. H. TORRINGTON, Esq.,
Principal of the Toronto
College of Music.

TORONTO COLLEGE OF MUSIC,
Pembroke St.

JAMES MILLS, M.A., LL.D.,
Principal of the Ontario
Agricultural College.

ONTARIO AGRICULTURAL COLLEGE,
Experimental Farm,
Guelph, Ont.